Prisha anand

ana Rita

   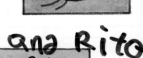

Riya

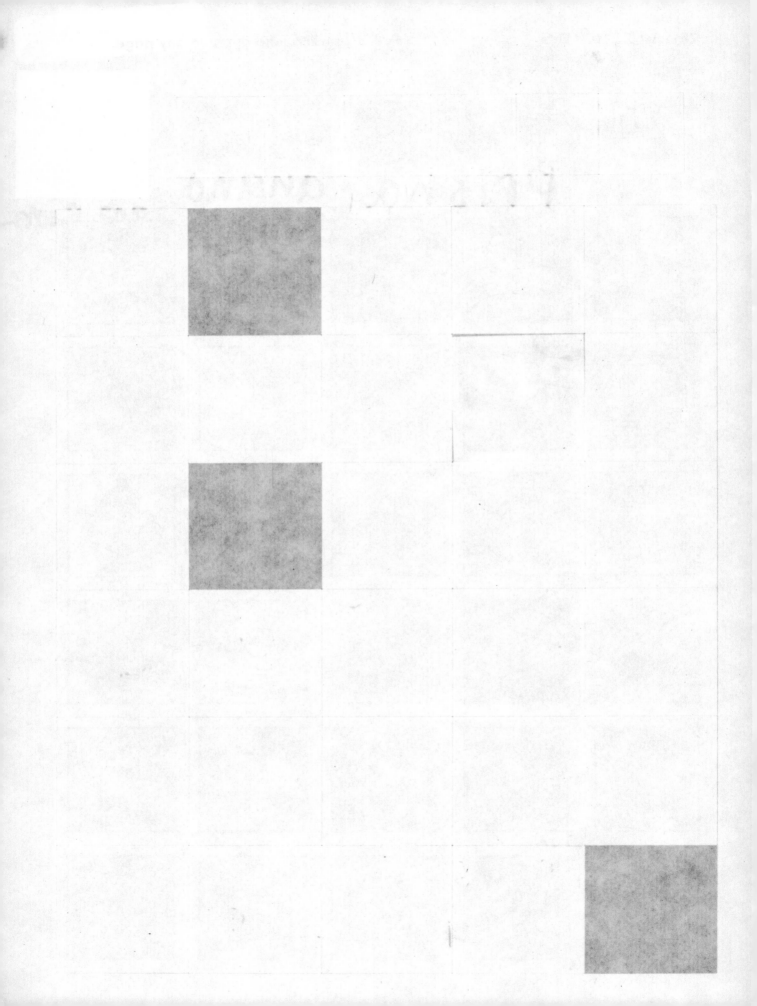

An Addition Riddle

 Add. Look at the code. Match your answers to the letters. Write the letters in the boxes.

code:

2	3	4	5	6	7	8	9	10
M	P	G	N	I	S	R	T	E

 Which season do kangaroos like best?

$$\begin{array}{r} 4 \\ +3 \\ \hline 7 \end{array} \quad \begin{array}{r} 1 \\ +2 \\ \hline 3 \end{array} \quad \begin{array}{r} 6 \\ +2 \\ \hline 8 \end{array} \quad \begin{array}{r} 2 \\ +4 \\ \hline 6 \end{array} \quad \begin{array}{r} 3 \\ +2 \\ \hline 5 \end{array} \quad \begin{array}{r} 2 \\ +2 \\ \hline 4 \end{array}$$

S	P	r	i	N	g

\-

$$\begin{array}{r} 4 \\ +5 \\ \hline 9 \end{array} \quad \begin{array}{r} 1 \\ +5 \\ \hline 6 \end{array} \quad \begin{array}{r} 1 \\ +1 \\ \hline 2 \end{array} \quad \begin{array}{r} 6 \\ +4 \\ \hline 10 \end{array}$$

t	i	m	e

!

Skill: using addition to complete a code

1

A Subtraction Riddle

Subtract. Look at the code. Match your answers to the letters. Write the letters in the boxes.

code:

4	6	5	2	8	7
E	B	R	L	Y	U

What fruit is always sad?

10 − 4	5 − 3	9 − 2	8 − 4	7 − 1	11 − 7	10 − 5	12 − 7	12 − 4
6	2	7	4	6	5	5	5	8
B	L	Y	E	B	R	R	R	Y

2

Add or subtract.
Color the spaces with
the answers:

7 - | YELLOW |

8 - | ORANGE |

9 - | BROWN |

10 - | BLACK |

$$5 + 2 = 7$$

$$16 - 8 = 8$$

$$14 - 5 = 9$$

$$7 + 3 = 10$$

$$6 + 4 = 10$$

$$11 - 4 = 7$$

$$6 + 4 = 10$$

$$15 - 5 = 10$$

$$2 + 6 = 8$$

$$5 + ? $$

$$12 - 5 = 7$$

$$14 - 6 = 8$$

$$16 - ? $$

$$8 + 2 = $$

$$15 - 7 = 8$$

$$7 + 2 = $$

$$9 - 9 = $$

$$9 - ? $$

Skill: using addition and subtraction to complete a picture

3

6/13

Number Families

◀ Add or subtract.

B.

$$\begin{array}{r} 6 \\ + 5 \\ \hline 11 \end{array} \qquad \begin{array}{r} 11 \\ - 5 \\ \hline 6 \end{array}$$

$$\begin{array}{r} 5 \\ + 6 \\ \hline 11 \end{array} \qquad \begin{array}{r} 11 \\ - 6 \\ \hline 5 \end{array}$$

A.

$$\begin{array}{r} 4 \\ + 5 \\ \hline 9 \end{array} \qquad \begin{array}{r} 9 \\ - 5 \\ \hline 4 \end{array}$$

$$\begin{array}{r} 5 \\ + 4 \\ \hline 9 \end{array} \qquad \begin{array}{r} 9 \\ - 4 \\ \hline 5 \end{array}$$

C.

$$\begin{array}{r} 6 \\ + 9 \\ \hline 15 \end{array} \qquad \begin{array}{r} 15 \\ - 9 \\ \hline 6 \end{array}$$

$$\begin{array}{r} 9 \\ + 6 \\ \hline 15 \end{array} \qquad \begin{array}{r} 15 \\ - 6 \\ \hline 9 \end{array}$$

D.

$$\begin{array}{r} 2 \\ + 9 \\ \hline 11 \end{array} \qquad \begin{array}{r} 11 \\ - 9 \\ \hline 2 \end{array}$$

$$\begin{array}{r} 9 \\ + 2 \\ \hline 11 \end{array} \qquad \begin{array}{r} 11 \\ - 2 \\ \hline 9 \end{array}$$

E.

$$\begin{array}{r} 3 \\ + 7 \\ \hline 10 \end{array} \qquad \begin{array}{r} 10 \\ - 7 \\ \hline 3 \end{array}$$

$$\begin{array}{r} 7 \\ + 3 \\ \hline 10 \end{array} \qquad \begin{array}{r} 10 \\ - 3 \\ \hline 7 \end{array}$$

4

13

Add or subtract. Color the shirts for each number family a different color.

Hint: There are four shirts for each family.

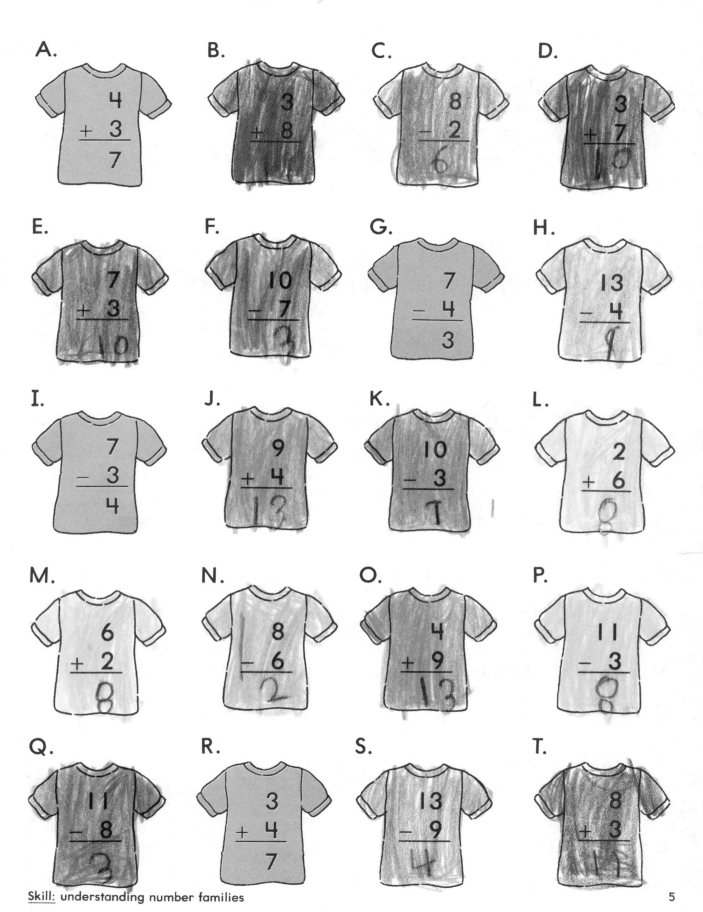

A.
$$4 + 3 = 7$$

B.
$$3 + 8$$

C.
$$8 - 2 = 6$$

D.
$$3 + 7 = 10$$

E.
$$7 + 3 = 10$$

F.
$$10 - 7 = 3$$

G.
$$7 - 4 = 3$$

H.
$$13 - 4 = 9$$

I.
$$7 - 3 = 4$$

J.
$$9 + 4 = 13$$

K.
$$10 - 3 = 7$$

L.
$$2 + 6 = 8$$

M.
$$6 + 2 = 8$$

N.
$$8 - 6 = 2$$

O.
$$4 + 9 = 13$$

P.
$$11 - 3 = 8$$

Q.
$$11 - 8 = 3$$

R.
$$3 + 4 = 7$$

S.
$$13 - 9 = 4$$

T.
$$8 + 3 = 11$$

Place Value

A number can also be called a digit.
A digit's value depends on its place.
For example,

	Hundreds	Tens	Ones
745 =	7	4	5

745 = 7 hundreds + 4 tens + 5 ones

745 = 700 + 40 + 5

	Hundreds	Tens	Ones
692 =	6	9	2

Fill in the blanks.

A. 692 = __6__ hundreds + __9__ tens + __2__ ones

B. 692 = __600__ + __40__ + __2__

C. The 6 is in the __Hundred__ place. Its value is __600__.

D. The 9 is in the __Tens__ place. Its value is __90__.

E. The 2 is in the __Ones__ place. Its value is __2__.

Put Me in My Place

⬦ Write each number.

5 tens and 4 ones = __54__

700 + 30 + 6 = __736__

---

1. 6 tens and 8 ones = __68__

2. 2 tens and 1 one = __21__

3. 5 tens and 0 ones = __50__

4. 4 hundreds, 3 tens, and 9 ones = __439__

5. 8 hundreds, 2 tens, and 5 ones = __825__

6. 3 hundreds, 0 tens, and 2 ones = __302__

7. 70 + 3 = __73__

8. 90 + 8 = __98__

9. 600 + 50 + 1 = __651__

10. 500 + 90 + 7 = __597__

11. 300 + 40 + 0 = __340__

12. 800 + 20 + 3 = __823__

Careful!

Skill: understanding place value

7

Greater Than, Less Than

▶ Professor Penguin's friends present:

"is greater than"   "is less than"

> **>** <   **<**

▶ Put the correct symbol between each set of numbers.

A. 53 $>$ 46   B. 27 $<$ 41

C. 16 $<$ 19   D. 80 $>$ 17

E. 514 $>$ 462   F. 368 $>$ 312

G. 531 $<$ 539   H. 902 $<$ 920

I. 673 $<$ 668   J. 699 $<$ 700

K. 480 $<$ 508   L. 711 $>$ 707

Skill: understanding the concepts greater than, less than

Place Value Practice

These are digits. A digit's value depends on its place.

6   2
    5
4   9
    8
3   0
1

A. Use the digits 3 and 7. Make a 2-digit number less than 48.

37

B. Use the digits 1 and 6. Make a 2-digit number greater than 52.

C. Use the digits 2 and 4. Make a 2-digit number less than 30.

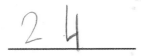

D. Use the digits 3 and 7. Make a 2-digit number greater than 64.

E. Use the digits 9, 4, and 6. Make two 2-digit numbers less than 50.

F. Use the digits 3, 1, and 9. Make two 2-digit numbers greater than 40.

G. Use the digits 3, 2, and 6. Make two 2-digit numbers less than 30.

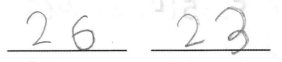

H. Use the digits 5, 3, and 6. Make two 2-digit numbers greater than 55.

Skills: understanding place value; greater than, less than

9

More Practice

🔺 Circle the number that is greater in each pair.

A.

510	(732)	(268)	705	(478)	912
(532)	723	150	(745)	476	(946)

🔺 Write the circled numbers from the least to the greatest.

B.

268	478	532	732	745	946

🔺 Write the circled number that has:

C. 2 in the hundreds place _268_

D. 7 in the tens place _478_

E. 4 in the hundreds place _478_

F. 5 in the ones place _745_

G. 6 in the ~~tens~~ *ones* place _946_

H. 6 in the ones place _946_

Skills: understanding place value; greater than/less than

A Puzzling Problem

Fill in the blanks of the puzzle with the correct answers.

		1. 3	6	2. 5		
3. 2	4. 1	8		5. 3	6. 7	7. 7
8. 1	6	2		9. 4	3	1
		10. 5	1	0		

ACROSS CLUES

1. 300 + 60 + 5
3. 2 hundreds, 1 ten, 8 ones
5. 300 + 70 + 7
8. 261 backwards
9. 400 + 30 + 1
10. 10 less than 580

DOWN CLUES

1. 3000 + 800 + 20 + 5
2. 10 more than 5330
3. 2 tens, 1 one
4. count by twos: 12, 14, ___?___
6. seventy-three
7. 9 less than 80

Add or Subtract

Add or subtract. Watch the signs.

A.
```
  24        75        72        68
+ 52      - 62      + 20      - 31
  76        13        92        3T
```

B.
```
  36        24        58        87
+ 43      - 12      + 21      - 24
  79        12        79        6B
```

C.
```
  18        86        21
+ 81      + 12      + 56
  99        98        1T
```

Watch the signs!

D.
```
  57        89        48
- 31      - 23      - 17
  26        66        31
```

12

Skill: adding and subtracting two-digit numbers

6/13

Add or subtract. Watch the signs.

A.
$$43 + 56 = 90$$
$$82 - 41 = 41$$
$$35 + 44 = 79$$
$$56 - 21 = 35$$

B.
$$27 + 32 = 59$$
$$50 + 29 = 79$$
$$78 - 35 = 43$$
$$62 + 25 = 87$$

C.
$$24 - 12 = 12$$
$$95 - 62 = 33$$
$$88 - 33 = 121$$
$$36 + 52 = 88$$

D.
$$19 + 40 = 59$$
$$54 + 43 = 97$$
$$96 - 32 = 64$$

E.
$$89 - 78 = 11$$
$$44 + 41 = 85$$
$$73 - 53 = 20$$

F.
$$56 + 12 = 68$$
$$67 - 41 = 100$$
$$43 + 46 = 89$$

A Number Puzzle

1. 6	2. 1		3. 3	4. 6
	5. 8	6. 1		3
7. 1		8. 2	9. 5	
10. 6	8		11. 9	2

Add or subtract. Fill in the blanks of the puzzle with the correct answers.

ACROSS CLUES

1. $\begin{array}{r} 43 \\ +24 \\ \hline 67 \end{array}$ 8. $\begin{array}{r} 56 \\ -31 \\ \hline 25 \end{array}$

3. $\begin{array}{r} 58 \\ -22 \\ \hline 36 \end{array}$ 10. $\begin{array}{r} 99 \\ -31 \\ \hline 68 \end{array}$

5. $\begin{array}{r} 64 \\ +23 \\ \hline 87 \end{array}$ 11. $\begin{array}{r} 41 \\ +51 \\ \hline 92 \end{array}$

DOWN CLUES

2. $\begin{array}{r} 36 \\ +42 \\ \hline 78 \end{array}$ 7. $\begin{array}{r} 68 \\ -52 \\ \hline 16 \end{array}$

4. $\begin{array}{r} 87 \\ -24 \\ \hline 63 \end{array}$ 9. $\begin{array}{r} 24 \\ +35 \\ \hline 59 \end{array}$

6. $\begin{array}{r} 21 \\ +51 \\ \hline 72 \end{array}$

14

Addition with Regrouping

1. Add.

```
   ı
   36
 + 47
   83
```

2. Add the ones.

tens	ones
ı	
3	6
+ 4	7
	3

Carry the one to the tens place.

3. Add the tens.

tens	ones
ı	
3	6
+ 4	7
8	3

2. Add.

```
   ı
   36
 + 47
   83
```

◀ Add the ones. Then add the tens.

A.

tens	ones
ı	
2	4
+	8
3	2

tens	ones
ı	
6	6
+	5
7	1

tens	ones
ı	
	8
+1	7
2	5

tens	ones
ı	
7	9
+	4
8	3

tens	ones
ı	
3	5
+	7
4	2

B.

```
   ı
   36
 + 27
   63
```

```
   ı
   28
 + 38
   66
```

```
   ı
   39
 + 42
   81
```

```
   ı
   19
 + 18
   37
```

```
   ı
   56
 + 26
   82
```

Practice Makes Perfect

◆ Add the ones. Then add the tens.

A.

tens	ones
4	3
+4	8
9	1

tens	ones
2	8
+4	3
7	1

tens	ones
2	7
+3	4
6	1

tens	ones
1	6
+7	8
9	4

tens	ones
5	7
+3	6
9	3

B.

```
   62        29        37        59        17
 + 19      +  6      + 49      + 28      + 18
   81        35        86        87        35
```

C.

```
            48        28
          +  4      + 55
            52        83
```

D.

```
            15        74
          + 29      +  9
            44        83
```

E.

```
             9        19
          + 41      + 33
            50        52
```

Check. Did you remember to regroup?

Skill: adding with regrouping (carrying)

Regrouping in Subtraction

To regroup in subtraction, you must change one group of ten into ten ones.

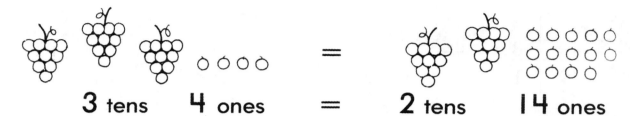

3 tens   **4** ones   =   **2** tens   **14** ones

Regroup 1 ten to show 10 more ones.

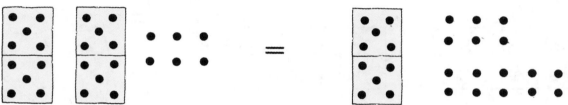

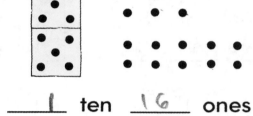

A. 2 tens **6** ones   =   ___1___ ten ___16___ ones

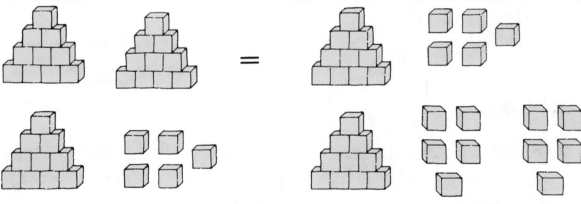

B. 3 tens **5** ones   =   ___2___ tens ___15___ ones

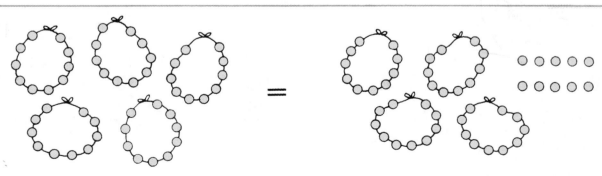

C. 5 tens **0** ones   =   ___4___ tens ___10___ ones

Subtraction with Regrouping 6/24

When you cannot subtract the bottom number from the top number, this is what you must do:

Subtract.

```
 5
 562
-14
 48
```

Regroup.

tens	ones
6̸ 5	2̸ 12
−1	4

Subtract the ones first.

tens	ones
6̸ 5	2̸ 12
−1	4
	8

Subtract the tens next.

tens	ones
6̸ 5	2̸ 12
−1	4
4	8

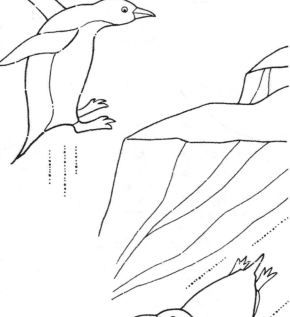

Subtract.

A.

tens	ones
8̸ 7	2̸ 12
−	6
7	6

tens	ones
7	1 2
−	2
6	9

tens	ones
8	0̸ 0
−	6
7	4

tens	ones
6	6̸ 0
−	8
5	2

tens	ones
5	1 1
−	3
4	8

B.

```
 65
-18
 47
```

```
 86
- 7
 79
```

```
4 53
-25
 28
```

```
 30
-17
 13
```

```
7 8 1
-34
 47
```

<u>Skill</u>: subtracting with regrouping (borrowing)

Regrouping Practice

Regroup. Subtract the ones. Subtract the tens.

A.
$$\begin{array}{r} {}^{3\ 14}\!\!\!44 \\ -\ 18 \\ \hline 26 \end{array}$$
$$\begin{array}{r} 51 \\ -\ 39 \\ \hline 12 \end{array}$$
$$\begin{array}{r} 56 \\ -\ \ 8 \\ \hline 48 \end{array}$$
$$\begin{array}{r} 94 \\ -\ 17 \\ \hline 77 \end{array}$$

B.
$$\begin{array}{r} 1\ 23 \\ -\ 17 \\ \hline 16 \end{array}$$
$$\begin{array}{r} 72 \\ -\ 26 \\ \hline 46 \end{array}$$
$$\begin{array}{r} 87 \\ -\ 68 \\ \hline 23 \end{array}$$
$$\begin{array}{r} 42 \\ -\ 34 \\ \hline 18 \end{array}$$

C.
$$\begin{array}{r} 42 \\ -\ \ 5 \\ \hline 37 \end{array}$$
$$\begin{array}{r} 35 \\ -\ 26 \\ \hline 18 \end{array}$$
$$\begin{array}{r} 82 \\ -\ 59 \\ \hline 33 \end{array}$$
$$\begin{array}{r} 60 \\ -\ 41 \\ \hline 29 \end{array}$$

D.
$$\begin{array}{r} 97 \\ -\ 59 \\ \hline \end{array}$$
$$\begin{array}{r} 75 \\ -\ \ 6 \\ \hline 69 \end{array}$$
$$\begin{array}{r} 91 \\ -\ 46 \\ \hline 55 \end{array}$$
$$\begin{array}{r} 62 \\ -\ 58 \\ \hline 12 \end{array}$$

E.
$$\begin{array}{r} 60 \\ -\ 29 \\ \hline 51 \end{array}$$
$$\begin{array}{r} 78 \\ -\ 19 \\ \hline 69 \end{array}$$

Don't forget to regroup.

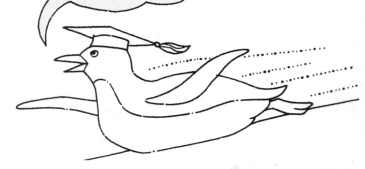

Skill: subtracting with regrouping (borrowing)

19

Bingo!

6/24

Add or subtract. Watch the signs!

A.
$$\begin{array}{r} \overset{7\ 13}{\cancel{83}} \\ -\ 15 \\ \hline 68 \end{array}$$
$$\begin{array}{r} 8 \\ +\ 43 \\ \hline 51 \end{array}$$
$$\begin{array}{r} 51 \\ -\ 28 \\ \hline 33 \end{array}$$
$$\begin{array}{r} 60 \\ -\ 49 \\ \hline 11 \end{array}$$
$$\begin{array}{r} 59 \\ +\ 14 \\ \hline 73 \end{array}$$

B.
$$\begin{array}{r} 29 \\ +\ 38 \\ \hline 57 \end{array}$$
$$\begin{array}{r} 74 \\ -\ 64 \\ \hline 10 \end{array}$$
$$\begin{array}{r} 67 \\ -\ 38 \\ \hline 29 \end{array}$$
$$\begin{array}{r} 28 \\ +\ 58 \\ \hline 80 \end{array}$$
$$\begin{array}{r} 60 \\ +\ 29 \\ \hline 84 \end{array}$$

C.
$$\begin{array}{r} 93 \\ -\ 77 \\ \hline 16 \end{array}$$
$$\begin{array}{r} 35 \\ +\ 7 \\ \hline 43 \end{array}$$
$$\begin{array}{r} 12 \\ +\ 49 \\ \hline 61 \end{array}$$
$$\begin{array}{r} 70 \\ -\ 22 \\ \hline 48 \end{array}$$
$$\begin{array}{r} 45 \\ -\ 8 \\ \hline 37 \end{array}$$

Find each of the answers on the game card. Put an X on each one. If your answers are correct, you will have bingo!

Bingo Card

51	75	6	67	89
61	83	86	25	67
37	68	47	29	23
73	5	10	74	42
16	81	48	11	52

Skill: adding and subtracting two-digit numbers to complete a game

Subtraction Check

6/24

Addition can be a way of checking your answer to a subtraction problem.

Subtract.

$$
\begin{array}{r}
\overset{5\ 12}{6\cancel{2}} \\
-48 \\
\hline
14
\end{array}
$$

Add.

$$
\begin{array}{r}
48 \\
+14 \\
\hline
62
\end{array}
$$

Check.

$$
\begin{array}{r}
62 \\
-48 \\
\hline
14
\end{array}
\qquad
\begin{array}{r}
48 \\
+14 \\
\hline
62
\end{array}
$$

Add or subtract. Then match each subtraction problem with its addition check by coloring the football and the helmet the same color.

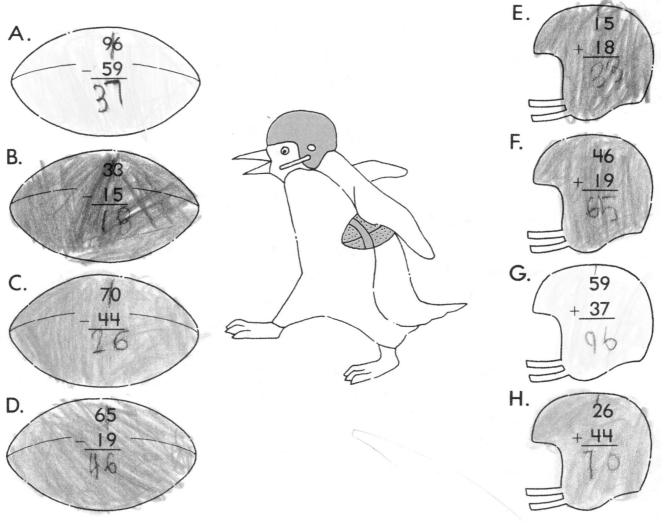

A.
$$
\begin{array}{r}
96 \\
-59 \\
\hline
37
\end{array}
$$

B.
$$
\begin{array}{r}
33 \\
-15 \\
\hline
18
\end{array}
$$

C.
$$
\begin{array}{r}
70 \\
-44 \\
\hline
26
\end{array}
$$

D.
$$
\begin{array}{r}
65 \\
-19 \\
\hline
46
\end{array}
$$

E.
$$
\begin{array}{r}
15 \\
+18 \\
\hline
33
\end{array}
$$

F.
$$
\begin{array}{r}
46 \\
+19 \\
\hline
65
\end{array}
$$

G.
$$
\begin{array}{r}
59 \\
+37 \\
\hline
96
\end{array}
$$

H.
$$
\begin{array}{r}
26 \\
+44 \\
\hline
70
\end{array}
$$

Skill: using addition to check answers in subtraction

21

Word Problems

Pam Teml

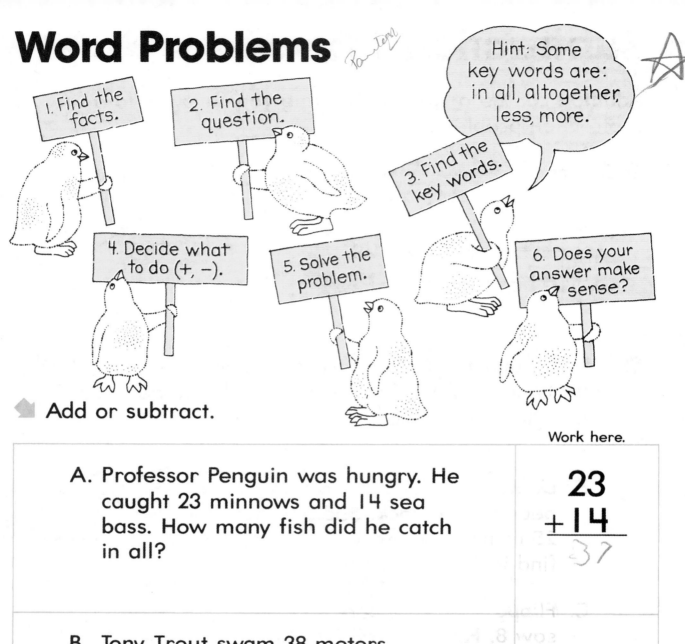

1. Find the facts.

2. Find the question.

3. Find the key words.

Hint: Some key words are: in all, altogether, less, more.

4. Decide what to do (+, −).

5. Solve the problem.

6. Does your answer make sense?

Add or subtract.

Work here.

Problem	Work
A. Professor Penguin was hungry. He caught 23 minnows and 14 sea bass. How many fish did he catch in all?	23 +14 37
B. Tony Trout swam 38 meters looking for food. His brother swam 26 meters. How much farther did Tony swim than his brother? Find the difference.	38 −26 12
C. Professor Penguin likes to watch the seagulls. One day he counted 45 seagulls. The next day he counted 36. How many seagulls did he see in all?	45 +36 81

Skill: using addition and subtraction to solve word problems

More Fish Tales!

Don't forget to watch for the key words.

◀ Add or subtract.

	Work here.
A. Professor Penguin found 12 starfish. Flipper found 16. How many starfish did they find in all?	$\begin{array}{r} 12 \\ +16 \\ \hline 28 \end{array}$
B. Dodie Dolphin found 31 old coins near a shipwreck. Sue Seal found 25 coins. How many coins did they find in all?	$\begin{array}{r} 31 \\ +25 \\ \hline 56 \end{array}$
C. Flipper saw 11 flounder. Susie saw 8. How many flounder did they see in all?	$\begin{array}{r} 11 \\ +8 \\ \hline 19 \end{array}$
D. On Saturday Dodie found 9 shells. On Sunday she found 16 shells. How many more shells did she find on Sunday than on Saturday?	$\begin{array}{r} 16 \\ -9 \\ \hline 7 \end{array}$
E. Professor Penguin saw 43 eels and 22 sharks. How many more eels than sharks did he see?	$\begin{array}{r} 43 \\ -22 \\ \hline 21 \end{array}$

Skill: using addition and subtraction to solve word problems

23

More Word Problems

 Add or subtract.

Work here.

A. There were 9 boys and 12 girls riding the merry-go-round. How many children were there in all?	$\begin{array}{r}1\\12\\+\ 9\\\hline 21\end{array}$
B. Terry had 96 balloons. He sold 58 balloons. How many balloons did he have left?	$\begin{array}{r}8\ \ 16\\\cancel{9}\ \cancel{6}\\-5\ 8\\\hline 3\ 8\end{array}$
C. Tom sold 37 hamburgers and 46 hot dogs at the carnival. How many sandwiches did he sell in all?	$\begin{array}{r}1\\37\\+46\\\hline 83\end{array}$
D. On Saturday 45 people went to the carnival. On Sunday there were 49 people at the carnival. How many people went to the carnival in all?	$\begin{array}{r}1\\45\\+49\\\hline 94\end{array}$
E. Marie sold 82 toy bears. She sold 65 toy giraffes. How many more bears were sold than giraffes?	$\begin{array}{r}7\ 12\\\cancel{8}\ \cancel{2}\\-65\\\hline 17\end{array}$

Skill: using addition and subtraction to solve word problems

Writing Word Problems

🔺 Fill in the blanks in the problems below. Then solve each problem. Write each answer in a number sentence.

Bill taught a bicycle safety class to **6** girls and **5** boys. How many children in all were there in the class?

$$6 + 5 = \boxed{11}$$

A. _____Katie_____ rode her bike _18_ miles on Monday and _17_ on Tuesday. How many miles did she ride in all?

$$18 + 17 = \boxed{35}$$

B. At the harbor, _violet_ counted _27_ speedboats and _20_ sailboats. How many boats did _____violet_____ count in all?

$$27 + 20 = \boxed{47}$$

C. _____lilly_____ planted the garden. She put in _10_ daisy plants and _17_ sunflowers. How many plants are in her garden?

$$10 + 17 = \boxed{27}$$

D. _____Daisy_____ is _2_ years old. Chris is _3_ years older. How old is Chris?

$$2 + 3 = \boxed{5}$$

Skills: completing word problems; using addition to solve word problems

25

Counting Coins

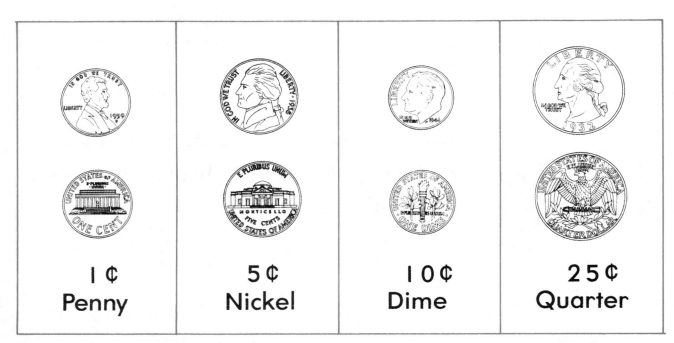

1¢ Penny	5¢ Nickel	10¢ Dime	25¢ Quarter

How many cents? Write the correct amount.

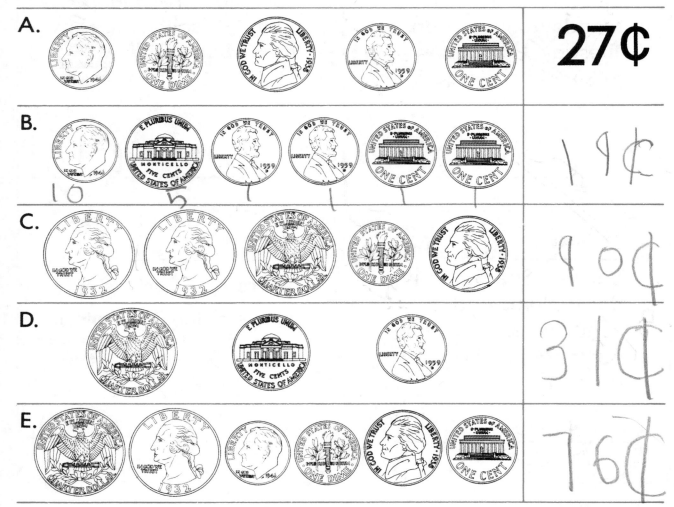

A. **27¢**

B. 19¢

C. 90¢

D. 31¢

E. 76¢

Skill: writing the value of a set of coins

How Much?

Look at the price of each toy. Look at each set of coins.
Circle the exact amount you would need to buy each toy.

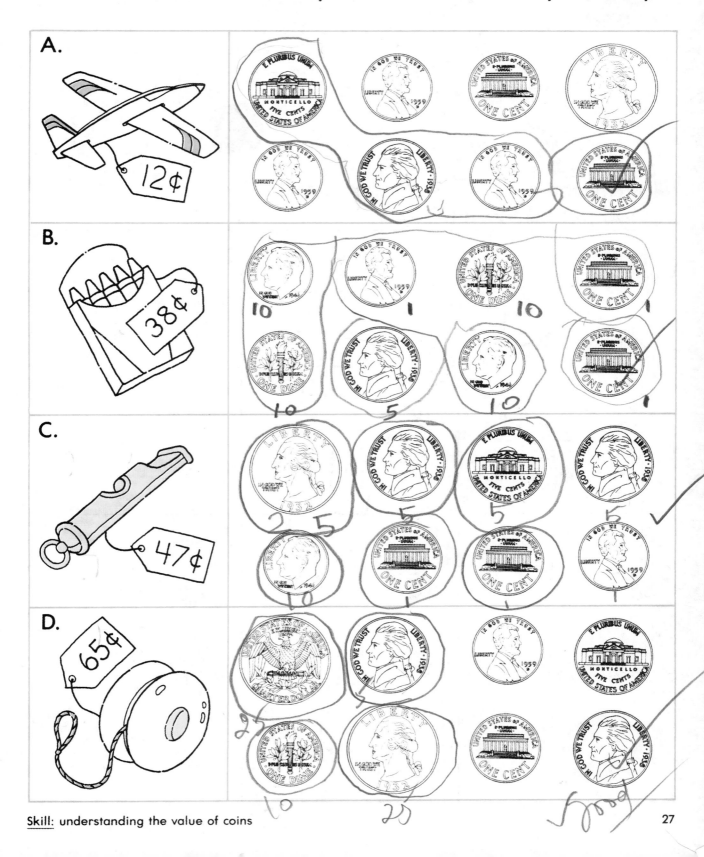

How Much Will You Spend?

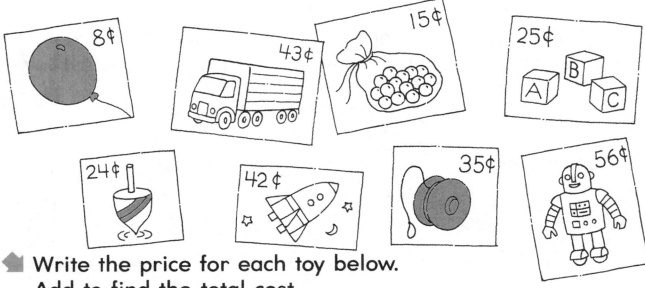

8¢   43¢   15¢   25¢

24¢   42¢   35¢   56¢

Write the price for each toy below.
Add to find the total cost.

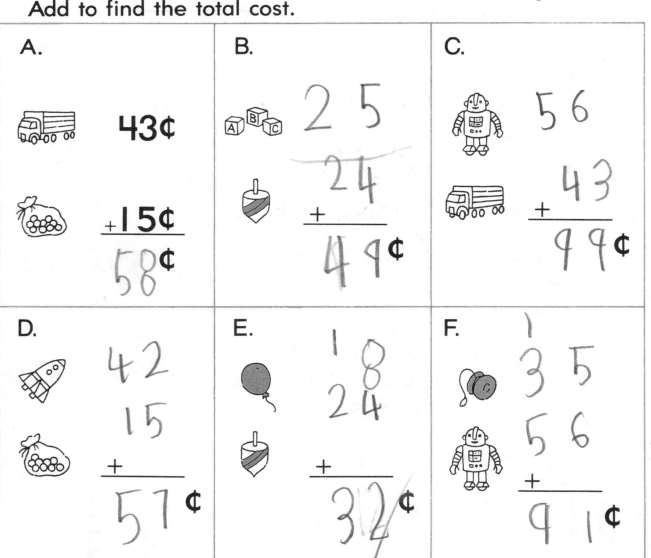

A.

43¢

+15¢

58¢

B.

2 5

2 4

+

4 9¢

C.

5 6

4 3

+

9 9¢

D.

4 2

1 5

+

5 7 ¢

E.

8

2 4

+

3 2 ¢

F.

3 5

5 6

+

9 1 ¢

28

Skill: using money to solve money problems

The Toy Store

Markers 43¢
STICKERS 49¢
76¢
CANDY 19¢
CARDS 59¢
37¢

Read each problem. Write the numbers. Add or subtract.

A. Monty bought a bag of candy and a race car. How much money did he spend?	19¢ + 76¢ 95¢
B. Allie had 62¢. She bought a box of markers. How much money does she have left?	6|2 – 4 3 1 9
C. Mark bought a card game. Dave bought a ball. How much more did Mark spend than Dave?	59 – M 37 22
D. Kris bought 2 packages of stickers. How much money did she spend?	4 9 + 4 9 9 8

Telling Time

The minute hand is on 12. The minute hand is the long hand.

The hour hand is on 4. The hour hand is the short hand.

It is 4 o' clock.

4:00

7/9

It is 4:30.

4:30

The hour hand is between 4 and 5.

The minute hand is on 6.

Look at each clock. Write the time.

A.

1:00

10:00

6:00

12:25

B.

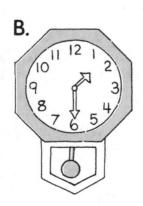

1:30

10:30

3:30

4:30

Skill: telling time on the hour and half hour

Give Me Five!

_____ 5
50 _____ 10
_____ 15
_____ 20
35 _____ _____
_____

It takes 5 minutes for the minute hand to move from one number to the next.

5, 10, 15 20...

◀ Count by fives. Write the numbers on the lines.

◀ Look at each clock. Write the time.

A.

7:10

8:30

6:45

B.

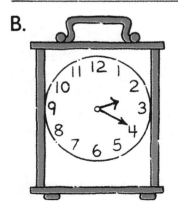

2:20

11:40

4:15

Skill: telling time — understanding 5 minute intervals   31

More Time

Draw a line from each clock to the correct time.

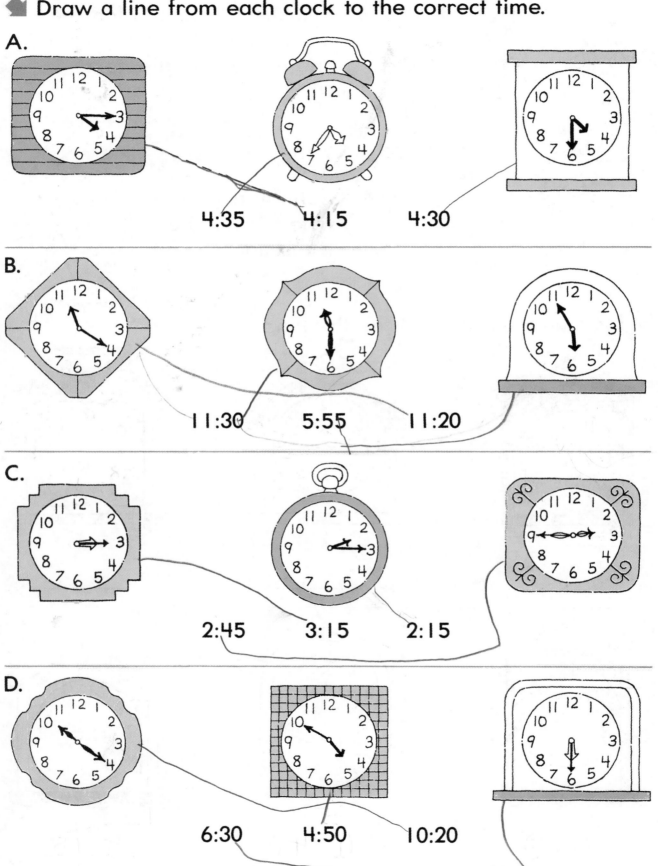

A.

4:35   4:15   4:30

B.

11:30   5:55   11:20

C.

2:45   3:15   2:15

D.

6:30   4:50   10:20

Skill: matching a clock to a given time

Time on Our Hands

Draw the hands on each clock, so they will show the correct time.

7/9

A.

7:30

2:00

1:15

B.

3:05

9:20

5:10

C.

6:25

8:45

11:00

Recognizing Shapes

7/10

🔸 How many corners? How many sides? Write the numbers.

rectangle

triangle

square

__4__ corners

__3__ corners

__4__ corners

__4__ sides

__3__ sides

__4__ sides

🔸 Put a C inside each circle.
Put a T inside each triangle.
Put an R inside each rectangle.
Put an S inside each square.

34

Find the hidden shapes in the picture.
Color:

yellow   red   blue   green

7/10

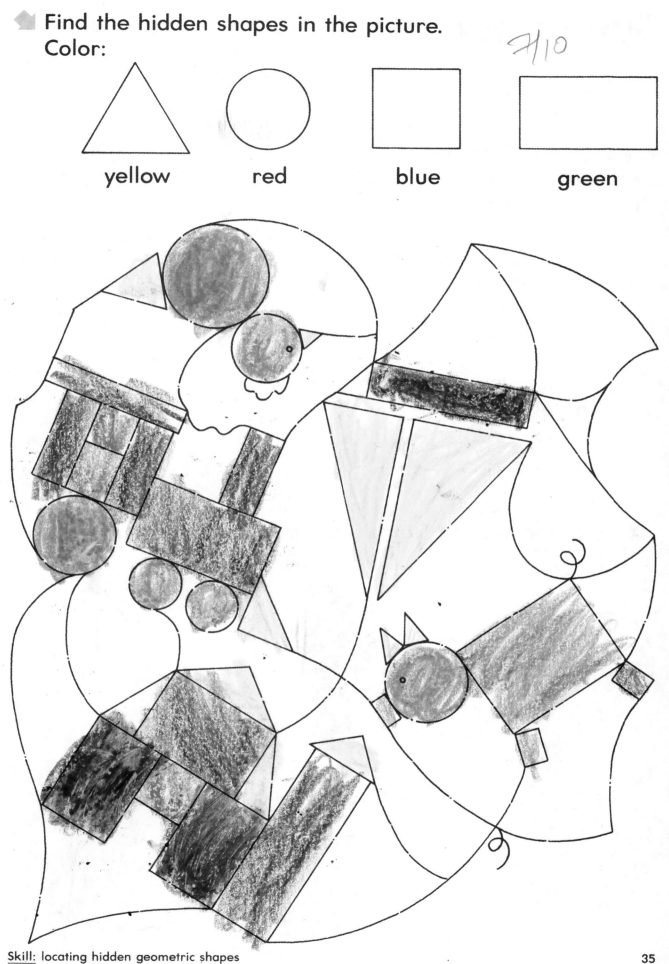

Symmetry

If you fold a shape on a line and the two parts match, the shape is symmetric.

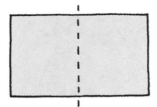

The line is called the line of symmetry.

The two parts match. It has symmetry.

710

⬢ Color the shapes that are symmetric.

A.

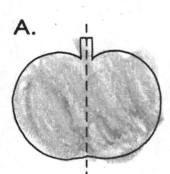

B.

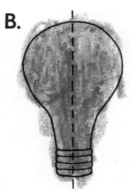

C.

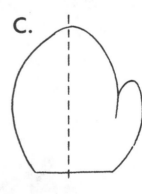

D.

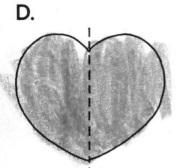

E.

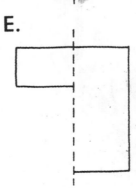

F.

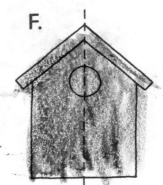

Skill: recognizing symmetric shapes

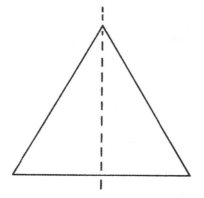

This triangle is
symmetric.

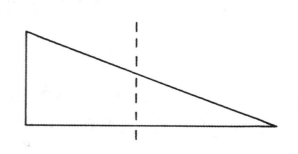

This triangle is
not symmetric.

7|10

 Circle the pictures that are symmetric.

A.

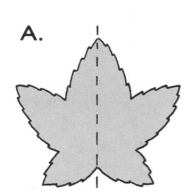

B.

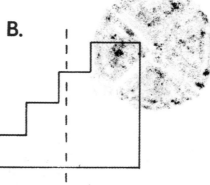

C.

D.

E.

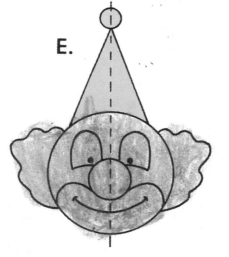

F.

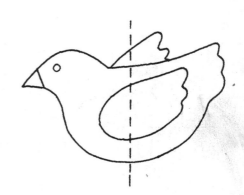

Equal Parts

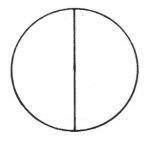

These shapes have equal parts.

These shapes do not have equal parts.

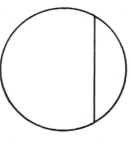

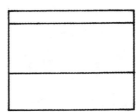

🔹 Color the shapes that have equal parts.

A.

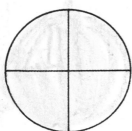

B.

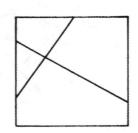

C.

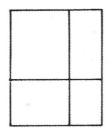

D.

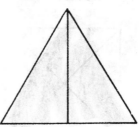

E.

F.

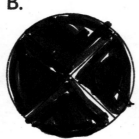

G.

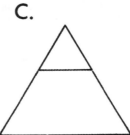

H.

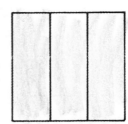

I.

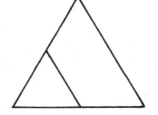

J.

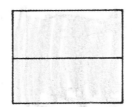

K.

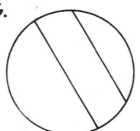

L.

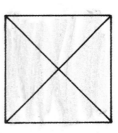

38

Fractions

 $\dfrac{1}{2}$ part
equal parts $=$ $\dfrac{1}{2}$ one half

 Color $\dfrac{1}{2}$ of each shape.

A. B. C.

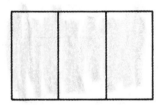 $\dfrac{1}{3}$ part
equal parts $=$ $\dfrac{1}{3}$ one third

 Color $\dfrac{1}{3}$ of each shape.

D. E. F.

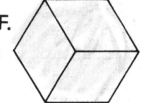

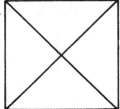 $\dfrac{1}{4}$ part
equal parts $=$ $\dfrac{1}{4}$ one fourth

 Color $\dfrac{1}{4}$ of each shape.

G. H. I.
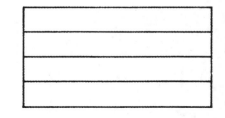

Skill: identifying equal parts 39

Halves, Thirds, Fourths

$$\frac{2 \text{ colored parts}}{3 \text{ equal parts}}$$

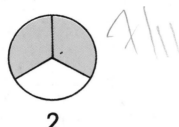

$$\frac{2}{3}$$

$$\frac{2 \text{ colored parts}}{4 \text{ equal parts}}$$

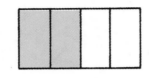

$$\frac{2}{4}$$

$$\frac{3 \text{ colored parts}}{4 \text{ equal parts}}$$

$$\frac{3}{4}$$

Circle the fraction for the colored area.

A.

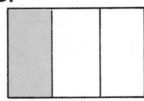

$$\frac{2}{3} \quad \left(\frac{2}{4}\right) \quad \frac{3}{4}$$

B.

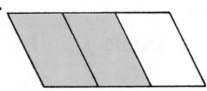

$$\frac{2}{3} \quad \frac{3}{4} \quad \frac{2}{4}$$

C.

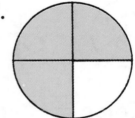

$$\frac{3}{4} \quad \frac{2}{3} \quad \frac{2}{4}$$

D.

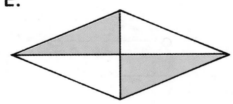

$$\frac{1}{3} \quad \frac{3}{4} \quad \frac{2}{3}$$

E.

$$\frac{2}{3} \quad \frac{3}{4} \quad \frac{2}{4}$$

F.

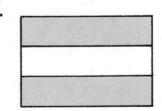

$$\frac{3}{4} \quad \frac{2}{4} \quad \frac{2}{3}$$

G.

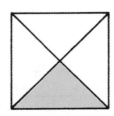

$$\frac{1}{3} \quad \frac{1}{4} \quad \frac{2}{4}$$

H.

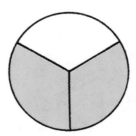

$$\frac{2}{4} \quad \frac{3}{4} \quad \frac{2}{3}$$

I.

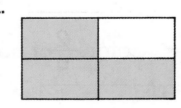

$$\frac{3}{4} \quad \frac{2}{3} \quad \frac{2}{4}$$

40

Color the correct number of equal parts for each fraction.

A.
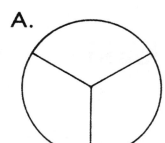
$\dfrac{2}{3}$

B.
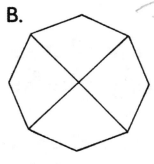
7/11
$\dfrac{3}{4}$

C.
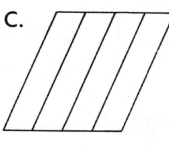
$\dfrac{2}{4}$

D.
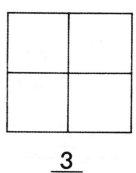
$\dfrac{3}{4}$

E.
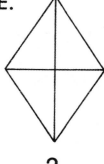
$\dfrac{2}{4}$

F.
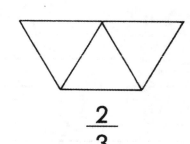
$\dfrac{2}{3}$

G.

$\dfrac{2}{4}$

H.
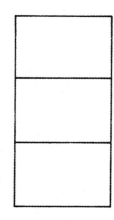
$\dfrac{2}{3}$

I.
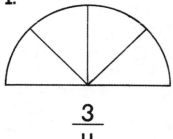
$\dfrac{3}{4}$

Skill: identifying fractions

41

Fraction Sets

 $\frac{1}{2}$ of the set is colored.

1 tells how many blocks are colored.
2 tells how many blocks in all.

Color the correct number of objects for each fraction.

A.

$\frac{1}{3}$

B.

$\frac{1}{2}$

C.

$\frac{1}{4}$

D.

$\frac{1}{3}$

E.

$\frac{1}{4}$

F.

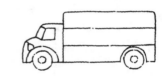

$\frac{1}{2}$

G.

$\frac{2}{4}$

H.

$\frac{2}{3}$

I.

$\frac{3}{4}$

Skill: identifying the correct number of objects for a given fraction

Inching Along

Cut out the ruler on page 47. Use it to measure each caterpillar to the nearest inch.

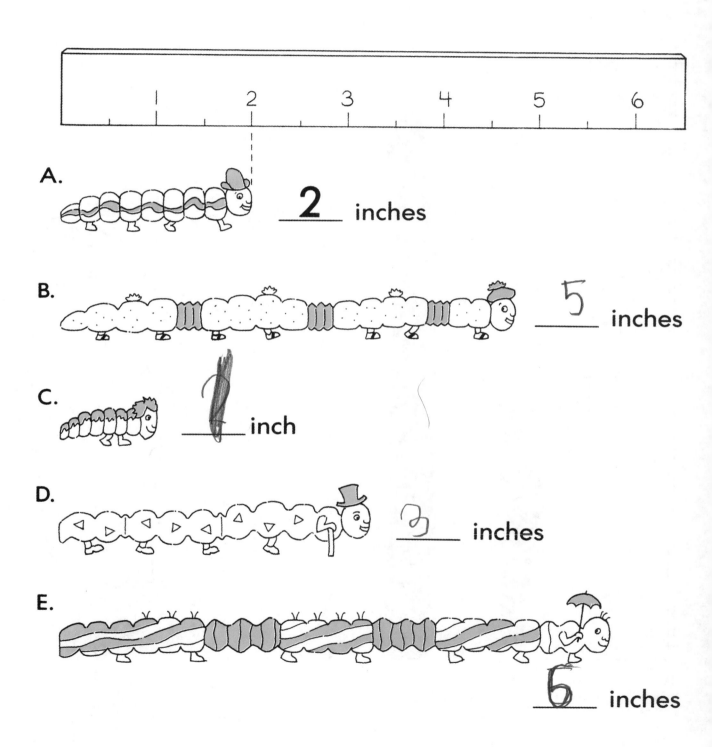

A. _____2_____ inches

B. _____5_____ inches

C. _____2_____ inch

D. _____3_____ inches

E. _____6_____ inches

How Tall?

Measure to the nearest inch.

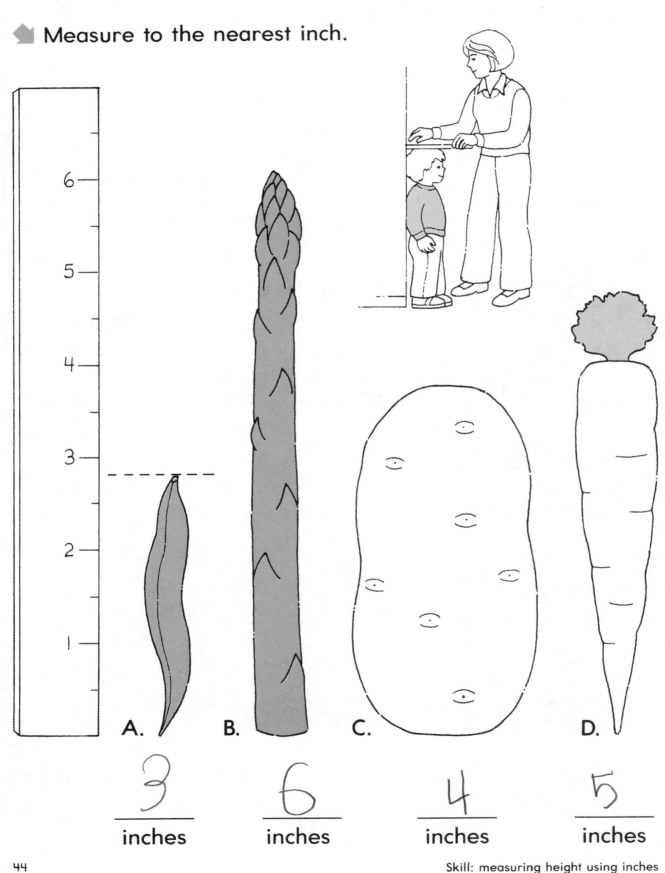

A. __3__
inches

B. __6__
inches

C. __4__
inches

D. __5__
inches

44

Measuring Centimeters

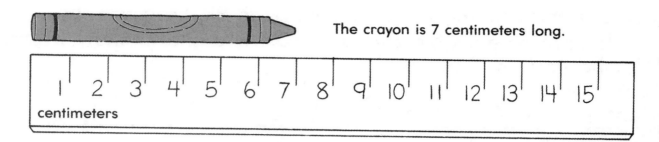

The crayon is 7 centimeters long.

🡄 Measure to the nearest centimeter.
Use the ruler on page 48.

A. _12_ centimeters

B. _3_ centimeters

C. _8_ centimeters

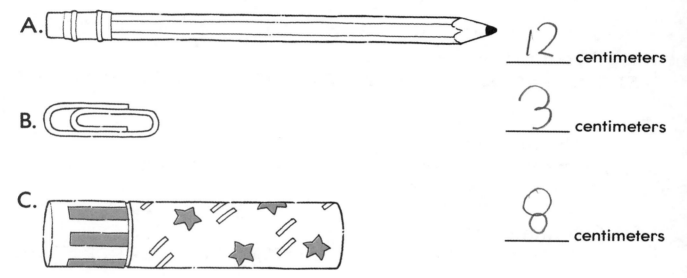

D. _13_ centimeters

E. _11_ centimeters

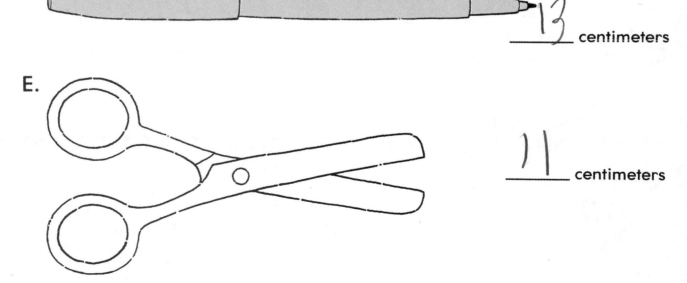

How Long?

Use the centimeter ruler from page 48. Measure the length for each piece of yarn. Draw a line to show where the yarn is to be cut.

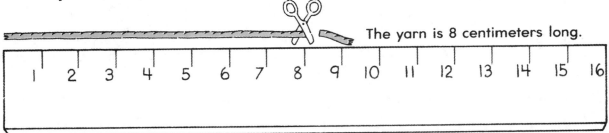

The yarn is 8 centimeters long.

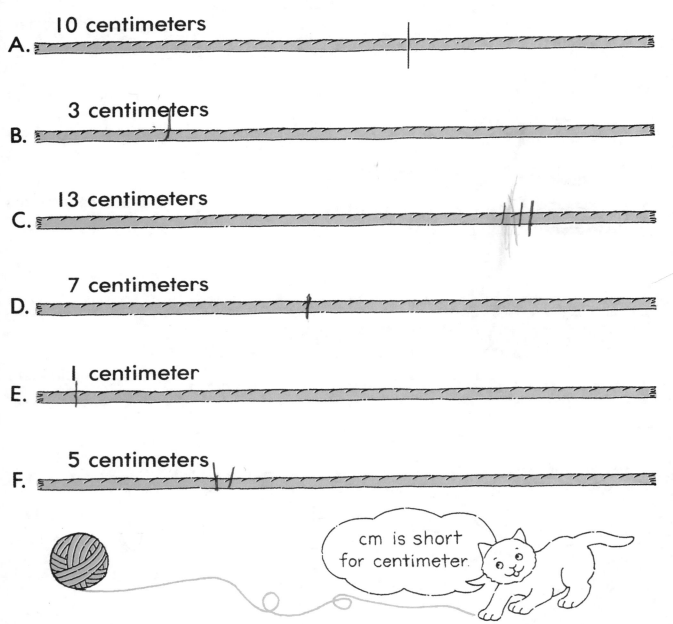

A. 10 centimeters

B. 3 centimeters

C. 13 centimeters

D. 7 centimeters

E. 1 centimeter

F. 5 centimeters

cm is short for centimeter.

Skill: measuring length using centimeters

How Far Did We Travel?

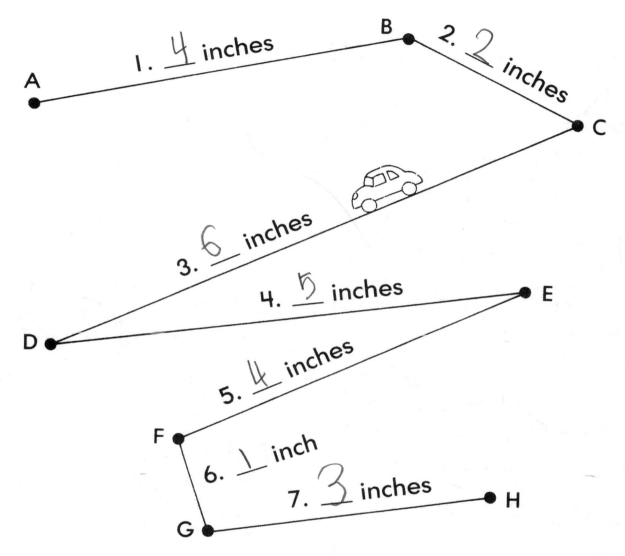

Use the inch ruler to measure the distance between points. Write the answers on the lines.

A — B   1. 4 inches

B — C   2. 2 inches

C — D   3. 6 inches

D — E   4. 5 inches

E — F   5. 4 inches

F — G   6. 1 inch

G — H   7. 3 inches

The car went from A to H.
How far did the car travel altogether?

8. 25 inches

Cut out the ruler.

```
|   1      2      3      4      5      6
inches
```

Dolly's Darling Dogs are going on a trip. Dolly needs travel boxes to fit each dog. Help Dolly by measuring each dog from nose to tail. Use the centimeter ruler.

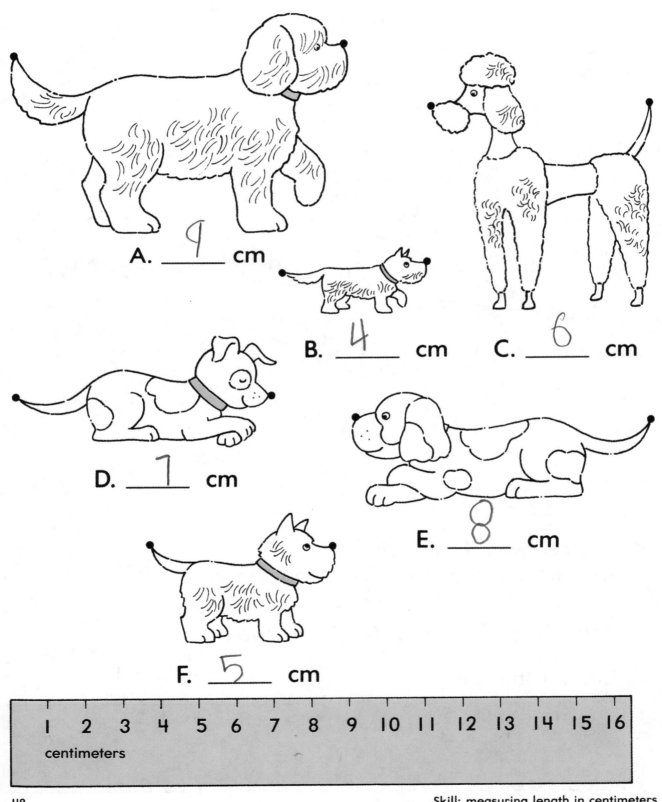

A. ___9___ cm

B. ___4___ cm

C. ___6___ cm

D. ___7___ cm

E. ___8___ cm

F. ___5___ cm

| 1 2 3 4 5 6 7 8 9 10 11 12 13 14 15 16 |
| centimeters |

Skill: measuring length in centimeters

Where Is the Bunny?

A bunny is hiding in one of the tents!
Use the centimeter ruler to measure the bottom of each tent. Write your answer on the line under each tent.

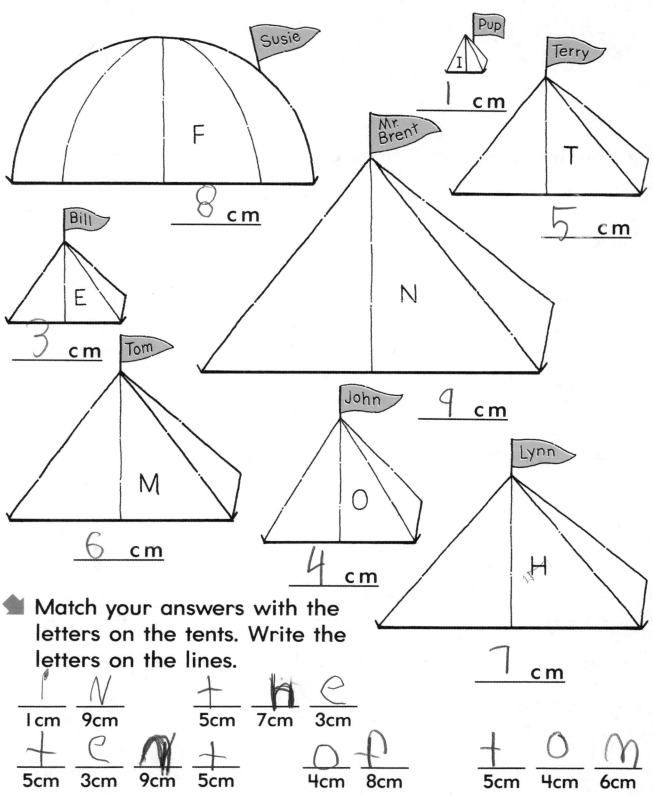

Susie
F
8 cm

Pup
I
1 cm

Terry
T
5 cm

Mr. Brent
N
9 cm

Bill
E
3 cm

Tom
M
6 cm

John
O
4 cm

Lynn
H
7 cm

Match your answers with the letters on the tents. Write the letters on the lines.

I	N		t	h	e
1cm	9cm		5cm	7cm	3cm

t	e	N	t		O	F
5cm	3cm	9cm	5cm		4cm	8cm

t	O	m
5cm	4cm	6cm

Skills: measuring length using centimeters; completing a code

49

Weight in Pounds

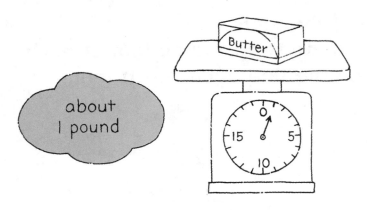

about
1 pound

I weigh 30 pounds.

◀ How many pounds? Write the answers.

A.

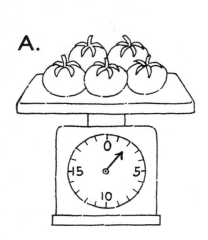

__2__ pounds

__10__ pounds

__4__ pounds

B.

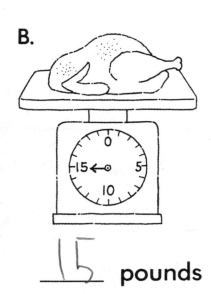

__15__ pounds

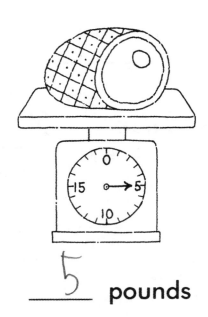

__5__ pounds

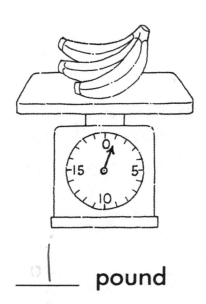

__1__ pound

50

<u>Skill</u>: understanding pounds

Weight in Kilograms

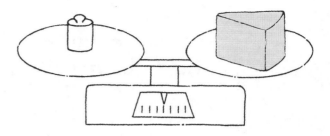 = 1 kilogram

How many kilograms? Write the answers.

A.

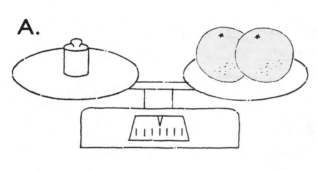

___1___ kilogram

___2___ kilograms

B.

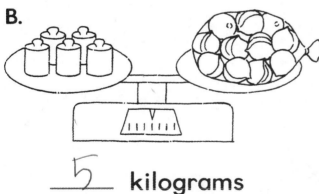

___5___ kilograms

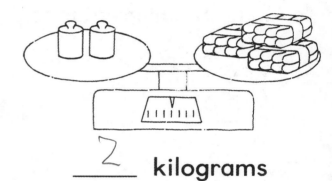

___4___ kilograms

C.

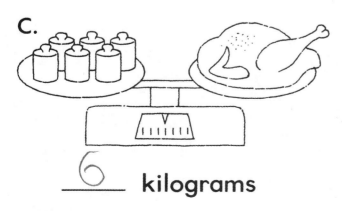

___6___ kilograms

___3___ kilograms

Liters

These containers hold about 1 liter.

Circle the things that hold **less** than 1 liter.

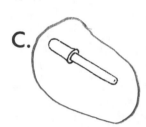

1 liter

A.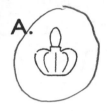

B.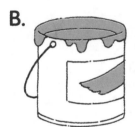

C.

D.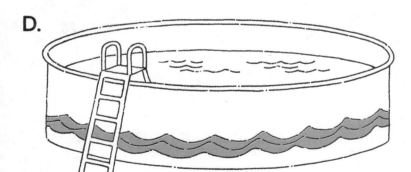

E.

F.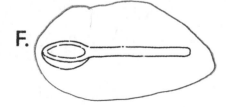

G.

52

Put an X on the things that hold **more** than 1 liter.

A.

B.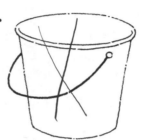

C.

D.

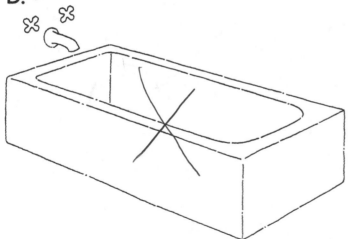

E.

F.

G.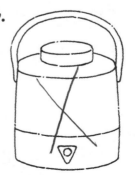

Skill: understanding liter measurement to estimate the capacity of a container   53

Quarts, Pints and Cups

1 quart = 2 pints = 4 cups

◀ Color the containers to show equal amounts.

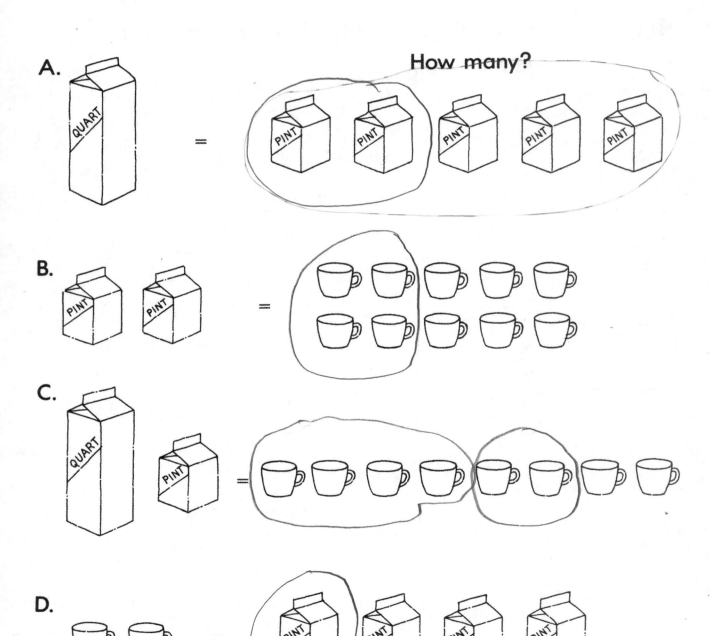

A.
How many?

B.

C.

D.

54

Skill: understanding quarts, pints and cups

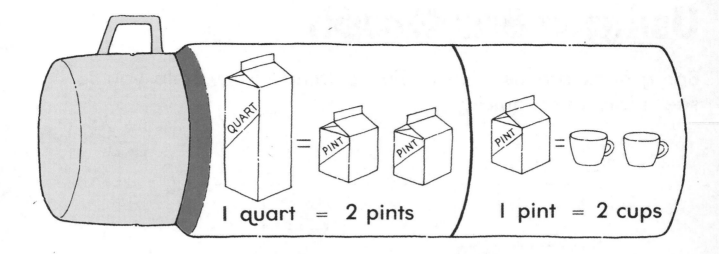

1 quart = 2 pints   1 pint = 2 cups

◀ Circle the amount in each row that is greater.

A.

     or

B.

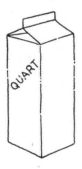   or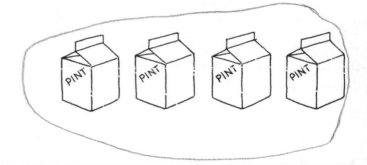

C.

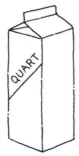   or

D.

Skill: understanding quarts, pints and cups

Using a Bar Graph

Bar graphs are used to compare things. They help you to see information quickly.

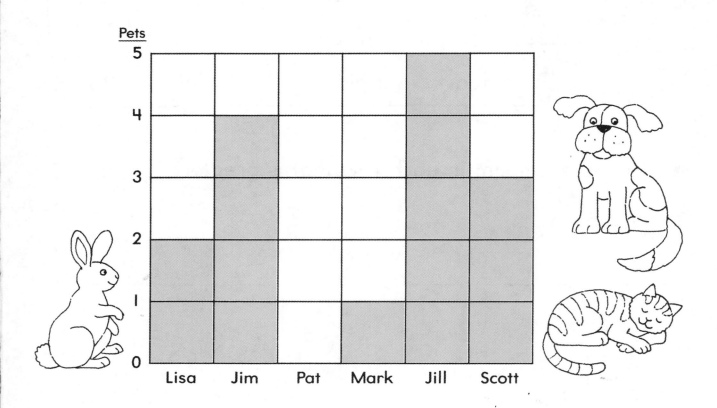

Pets

◀ Look at the bar graph. Fill in the answers below.

A. Jim has __4__ pets.

Jill has __5__ pets.

<u>Jim</u> has less.

B. Lisa has __2__ pets.

Scott has __3__ pets.

__Scott__ has more.

C. Mark has __1__ pet.

Pat has __0__ pets.

__Mark__ has more.

D. __Jim__ has 4 pets.

__Scott__ has 3 pets.

__Scott__ has less.

Skills: reading a bar graph; comparing information

Make Your Own Bar Graph

◄ Color the squares to show how many.

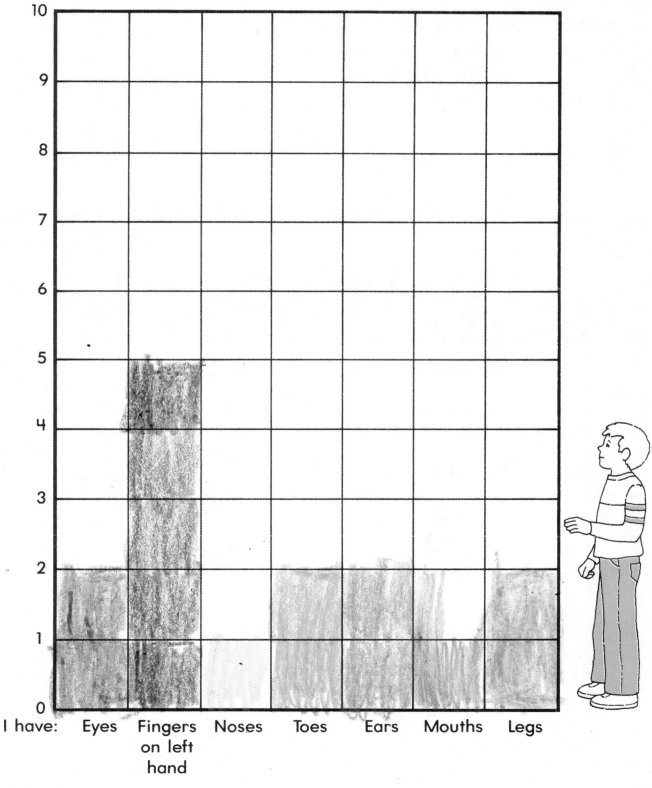

I have: Eyes Fingers Noses Toes Ears Mouths Legs
              on left
                hand

Reading Tables

Peter Penguin read a book about animals. Here is what he read:

A cheetah can run about 70 miles per hour (or 70 mph).

A bobcat can run about 65 mph.

An ostrich can run about 40 mph.

A dog can run about 35 mph.

A giraffe can run about 30 mph.

Use the information above to fill in the blanks in the table.

Running Speeds of Some Animals

Animal	Speed
cheetah	70 mph
bobcat	65 mph
ostrich	40 mph
dog	35 mph
giraffe	30 mph

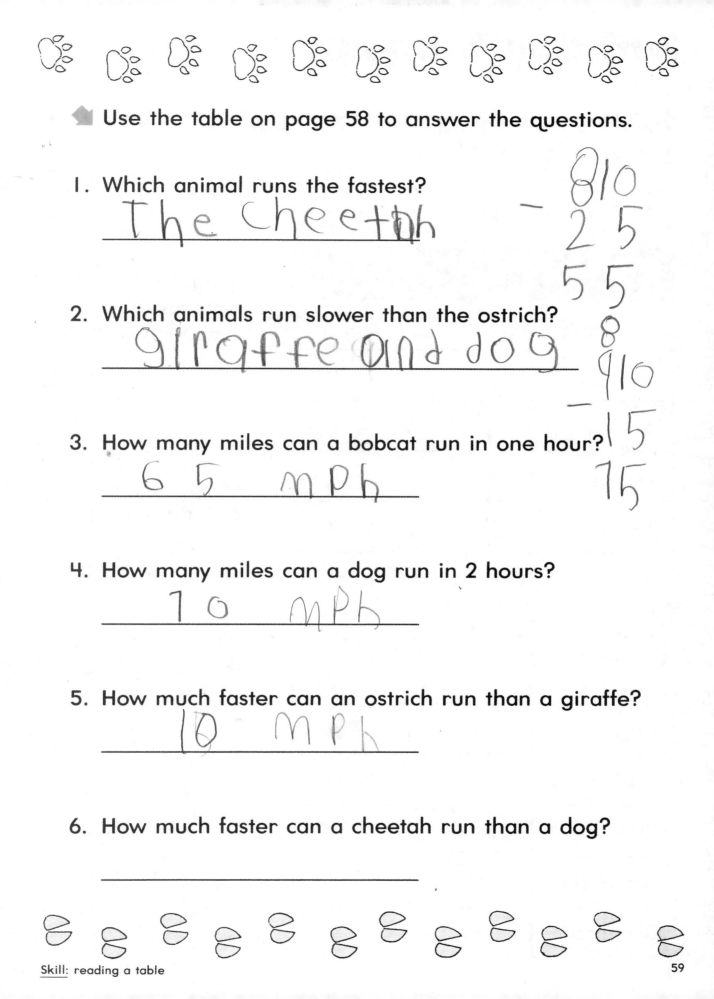

Use the table on page 58 to answer the questions.

1. Which animal runs the fastest?

   The Cheetah

2. Which animals run slower than the ostrich?

   giraffe and dog

3. How many miles can a bobcat run in one hour?

   65 mph

4. How many miles can a dog run in 2 hours?

   70 mph

5. How much faster can an ostrich run than a giraffe?

   10 mph

6. How much faster can a cheetah run than a dog?

   _____

Birthday Penguins

Fill in the answer in each blank square in the table. Then answer the questions.

Birthdays			
Month	Girl Penguins	Boy Penguins	How many in all?
January	5	2	7
February	3	6	9
March	4	1	5
April	7	2	9
May	4	4	8
June	4	6	10
July	0	2	2
August	1	4	5
September	2	3	5
October	2	6	8
November	5	2	7
December	3	6	9

1. How many boy penguins have birthdays in October?

   8

2. How many girl penguins have birthdays in April?

   9

3. Which month has the most birthdays?

   June

60

ANSWERS

Page 1
7, 3, 8, 6, 5, 4
9, 6, 2, 10
Spring-Time!

Page 2
6, 2, 7, 4, 6, 4, 5, 5, 8
Blueberry

Page 3
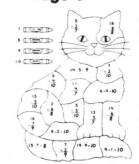

Page 4

Page 5
A. 7   B. 11   C. 6   D. 10
E. 10   F. 3   G. 3   H. 9
I. 4   J. 13   K. 7   L. 8
M. 8   N. 2   O. 13   P. 8
Q. 3   R. 7   S. 4   T. 11
Number Families:
A, G, I, R
B, P, Q, T
C, L, M, N
D, E, F, K
H, J, O, S

Page 6
A. 6, 9, 2
B. 600, 90, 2
C. hundreds, 600
D. tens, 90
E. ones, 2

Page 7
1. 68   2. 21
3. 50   4. 439
5. 825   6. 302
7. 73   8. 98
9. 651   10. 597
11. 340   12. 823

Page 8
A. 53 > 46   B. 27 < 41
C. 16 < 19   D. 80 > 17
E. 514 > 462   F. 368 > 312
G. 531 < 539   H. 902 < 920
I. 673 > 668   J. 699 < 700
K. 480 < 508   L. 711 > 707

Page 9
A. 37   E. 46, 49
B. 61   F. 91, 93
C. 24   G. 23, 26
D. 73   H. 63, 65

Page 10
A. 532, 732, 268, 745, 478, 946
B. 268, 478, 532, 732, 745, 946
C. 268
D. 478
E. 478
F. 745
G. 268
H. 946

Page 11

Page 12
A. 76, 13, 92, 37
B. 79, 12, 79, 63
C. 99, 98, 77
D. 26, 66, 31

Page 13
A. 99, 41, 79, 35
B. 59, 79, 43, 87
C. 12, 33, 55, 88
D. 59, 97, 64
E. 11, 85, 20
F. 68, 26, 89

Page 14

Page 15
A. 32, 71, 25, 83, 42
B. 63, 66, 81, 37, 82

Page 16
A. 91, 71, 61, 94, 93
B. 81, 35, 86, 87, 35
C. 52, 83
D. 44, 83
E. 50, 52

Page 17
A. 1 ten   16 ones
B. 2 tens   15 ones
C. 4 tens   10 ones

Page 18
A. 76, 69, 74, 57, 48
B. 47, 79, 28, 13, 47

Page 19
A. 26, 12, 48, 77
B. 6, 46, 19, 8
C. 37, 9, 23, 19
D. 38, 69, 45, 4
E. 31, 59

Page 20
A. 68, 51, 23, 11, 73
B. 67, 10, 29, 86, 89
C. 16, 42, 61, 48, 37

Bingo Card

5	75	6	87	84
88	83	86	25	87
66	66	47	29	28
78	5	10	74	42
15	81	46	71	52

Page 21
A. 37   E. 33
B. 18   F. 65
C. 26   G. 96
D. 46   H. 70
A-G, B-E,
C-H, D-F

Page 22
A. 37
B. 12
C. 81

Page 24
A. 21
B. 38
C. 83
D. 94
E. 17

Page 26
A. 27¢
B. 19¢
C. 90¢
D. 31¢
E. 76¢

Page 23
A. 28
B. 56
C. 19
D. 7
E. 21

Page 27

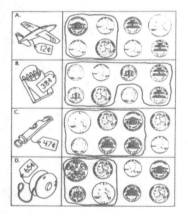

Page 28
A. 58¢   B. 49¢   C. 99¢
D. 57¢   E. 32¢   F. 91¢

Page 31
A. 7:10, 8:30, 5:45
B. 2:20, 11:40, 4:15

Page 32

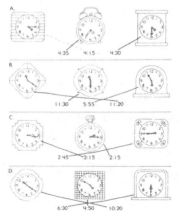

Page 29
A. 95¢   B. 19¢
C 22¢   D. 98¢

Page 30
A. 1:00, 10:00, 6:00, 5:00
B. 1:30, 10:30, 3:30, 9:30

Page 33

A. 7:30   2:00   1:15

B. 3:05   9:20   5:10

C. 6:25   8:45   11:00

Page 34

Recognizing Shapes

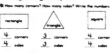

How many corners? How many sides? Write the numbers.

rectangle   triangle   square

4 corners   3 corners   4 corners
4 sides   3 sides   4 sides

Put a C inside each circle
Put a T inside each triangle
Put an R inside each rectangle
Put an S inside each square

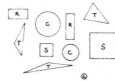

Page 36
A., B., D., F.
are symmetric

Page 37
A., C., D., E.
are symmetric

Page 39

Fractions

$\frac{1}{2}$ part $\frac{1}{2}$ one half
equal parts

Color $\frac{1}{2}$ of each shape.

A.   B.   C.

$\frac{1}{3}$ part $\frac{1}{3}$ one third
equal parts

Color $\frac{1}{3}$ of each shape.

D.   E.   F.

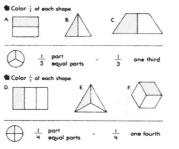

$\frac{1}{4}$ part $\frac{1}{4}$ one fourth
equal parts

Color $\frac{1}{4}$ of each shape.

G.   H.   I.

Page 38
A., B., D., F., H., I., L.

Page 40

A. $\frac{2}{4}$ B. $\frac{2}{3}$ C. $\frac{3}{4}$

D. $\frac{1}{3}$ E. $\frac{2}{4}$ F. $\frac{2}{3}$

G. $\frac{1}{4}$ H. $\frac{2}{3}$ I. $\frac{3}{4}$

Page 41

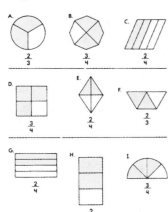

A. $\frac{2}{3}$ B. $\frac{3}{4}$ C. $\frac{2}{4}$

D. $\frac{3}{4}$ E. $\frac{2}{4}$ F. $\frac{2}{3}$

G. $\frac{2}{4}$ H. $\frac{2}{3}$ I. $\frac{3}{4}$

Page 42

A. $\frac{1}{3}$ B. $\frac{1}{2}$ C. $\frac{1}{4}$

D. $\frac{1}{3}$ E. $\frac{1}{4}$ F. $\frac{1}{2}$

G. $\frac{2}{4}$ H. $\frac{2}{4}$ I. $\frac{3}{4}$

Page 43
inches:
A. 2   B. 5
C. 1   D. 3
E. 6

Page 44
inches:
A. 3   B. 6
C. 4   D. 5

Page 45
centimeters:
A. 12
B. 3
C. 8
D. 13
E. 10

Page 47
inches:
1. 4
2. 2
3. 6
4. 5
5. 4
6. 1
7. 3
8. 25

63

Page 48
centimeters:
- A. 9
- B. 4
- C. 6
- D. 7
- E. 8
- F. 5

Page 49

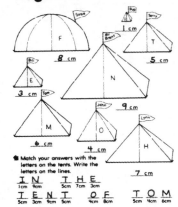

Match your answers with the letters on the tents. Write the letters on the lines.

I N   T H E
1cm 9cm   5cm 7cm 3cm

T E N T   O F   T O M
5cm 3cm 9cm 5cm   4cm 8cm   5cm 4cm 6cm

Page 50
pounds:
- A. 2, 10, 4
- B. 15, 5, 1

Page 51
kilograms:
- A. 1, 2
- B. 5, 4
- C. 6, 3

Page 52
A., C., E., F.

Page 53
B., D., G.

Page 54
- A. 2 pints
- B. 4 cups
- C. 6 cups
- D. 1 pint

Page 55
- A. 3 cups
- B. 4 pints
- C. 1 quart and 2 pints
- D. 3 cups and 1 pint

Page 56
- A. 4, 5, Jim
- B. 2, 3, Scott
- C. 1, 0, Mark
- D. Jim, Scott, Scott

Page 58

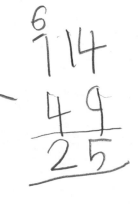

Running Speeds of Some Animals	
Animal	Speed
cheetah	70 mph
bobcat	65 mph
ostrich	40 mph
dog	35 mph
giraffe	30 mph

Page 59
1. cheetah
2. dog, giraffe
3. 65 miles
4. 70 miles
5. 10 miles per hour
6. 35 miles per hour

Page 60

Birthdays			
Month	Girl Penguins	Boy Penguins	How many in all?
January	5	2	7
February	3	6	9
March	4	1	5
April	7	2	9
May	4	4	8
June	4	6	10
July	0	2	2
August	1	4	5
September	2	3	5
October	2	6	8
November	5	2	7
December	3	6	9

1. How many boy penguins have birthdays in October? 6

2. How many girl penguins have birthdays in April? 7

3. Which month has the most birthdays? June

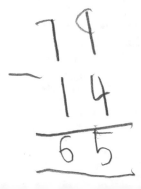

REWARD STICKERS